SHARI FRANKE'S LIFE BEYOND THE SPOTLIGHT

A Biography of Resilience, Creativity, and Transformation

VICTORIA PRESS

This book is a work of biography. While the author has made every effort to ensure the accuracy of the information contained within, certain details have been reconstructed from the author's interpretation of publicly available resources, interviews, and commentary.

Disclaimer

This book is an independent and unauthorized biography of Shari Franke. It is not affiliated with, endorsed by, or authorized by Shari Franke or her representatives. All opinions expressed herein are solely those of the author.

The content is based on publicly available information, interviews, and author research, and reasonable efforts have been made to ensure its accuracy. However, the author and publisher make no claims or guarantees regarding the completeness or accuracy of the information presented.

The reader is encouraged to approach the material with an open mind and verify information independently if necessary.

TABLE OF CONTENTS

INTRODUCTION 6

Shari Franke: From YouTube Stardom to Personal Empowerment 6

Why This Biography Matters.. 7

1. ROOTS OF THE FRANKE FAMILY 10

Growing Up in Utah 10

Family Traditions and Values 11

2. THE BIRTH OF 8 PASSENGERS 14

Entering the Spotlight.. 14

Family Dynamics on Camera.. 15

3. SHARI'S CHILDHOOD BEHIND THE SCENES...................18

Balancing Public and Private Life 18

Early Signs of Independence.. 19

4. THE RISE OF 8 PASSENGERS.......................................22

Capturing Family Moments 22

Shari's Role as the Eldest Sibling....................................... 23

5. THE CHALLENGES OF INTERNET FAME 26

Public Scrutiny and Online Criticism.................................. 26

Coping with Pressure and Expectations 27

6. FINDING HER VOICE...30

Expressing Identity Amid the Spotlight 30

Moments of Vulnerability and Growth.............................. 31

7. LEAVING THE NEST **34**

Pursuing Higher Education 34

Life Beyond the Camera.............................. 35

8. REDEFINING RELATIONSHIPS.................................**38**

Navigating Family Tensions.............................. 38

The Decision to Speak Out.............................. 39

9. THE HOUSE OF MY MOTHER: A JOURNEY OF REFLECTION............**42**

Shari's Inspirational Debut Book.............................. 42

Personal Growth Through Writing.............................. 43

10. BUILDING A LIFE OF INDEPENDENCE **46**

Academic Achievements and Goals.............................. 46

The Shift Toward Advocacy and Awareness 47

11. FAITH, CREATIVITY, AND PURPOSE.................................**50**

Shari's Personal Beliefs and Their Influence.............................. 50

Exploring Her Artistic and Creative Side 51

12. EMPOWERING OTHERS.................................**54**

Messages of Hope and Resilience 54

Inspiring Young Women to Embrace Change 55

13. THE IMPACT OF HER JOURNEY **58**

Reflections on Fame, Family, and Freedom 58

14. LOOKING AHEAD **60**

Shari's Vision for the Future 60

The Ongoing Story of Transformation 61

INTRODUCTION

Shari Franke: From YouTube Stardom to Personal Empowerment

Shari Franke's story is one of transformation and resilience. As a member of the Franke family, she was catapulted into the public eye through the widely popular YouTube channel, *8 Passengers*. Millions of viewers tuned in daily to witness the ups and downs of her family life, from heartwarming sibling moments to the challenges of growing up under the constant gaze of the internet. Shari was not just a participant in the channel's success but a central figure whose personality and authenticity captured the hearts of many.

Yet, Shari's journey extends far beyond her role in the family's digital narrative. While her early years were defined by the YouTube channel's rapid rise, her later decisions to step away from the spotlight marked the beginning of a transformative path toward independence and self-discovery. It wasn't merely about leaving the channel or moving away from her family—it was about redefining her identity and claiming her voice in a world that often attempted to tell her story for her.

In the years following her departure from the YouTube realm, Shari has pursued education, cultivated her creativity, and embraced the power of storytelling. Her debut book, *The House of My Mother*, provides a poignant window into her reflections on family, faith, and the complexities of personal growth. Through it all, Shari has emerged as a role model for young adults navigating their own journeys of self-discovery and empowerment.

Why This Biography Matters

This biography is more than a recounting of events—it is an exploration of themes that resonate deeply with anyone who has ever faced challenges in their pursuit of identity and purpose. Shari Franke's life provides a lens through which we can examine the pressures of fame, the trials of family dynamics, and the triumphs of resilience and creativity.

In an era when the line between private life and public persona grows increasingly blurred, Shari's story offers a valuable perspective on navigating the complexities of modern life. Her experiences shed light on the toll of living under constant scrutiny and the courage required to break free from societal expectations.

Moreover, this biography seeks to honor Shari's journey while addressing the universal human themes of growth, transformation, and the pursuit of meaning. It is not merely a reflection of her life but an invitation for readers to reflect on their own challenges and triumphs. Whether you are a fan of Shari, a curious observer of the digital age, or someone in search of inspiration, her story promises to leave a lasting impression.

This book is for anyone who has ever felt the weight of expectations, the pull of their dreams, or the need to redefine their place in the world. It is a celebration of resilience and the enduring human spirit—a testament to the idea that no matter where we begin, the journey to empowerment is always worth taking.

1. ROOTS OF THE FRANKE FAMILY

Growing Up in Utah

Shari Franke's journey begins in the heart of Utah, a state known for its breathtaking landscapes and deeply rooted cultural and religious traditions. Nestled among the towering mountains and serene valleys, Utah was not just a geographical location for the Franke family but a foundation for their way of life. Shari and her siblings grew up in a close-knit environment, where the sense of community was as strong as the natural beauty surrounding them.

Life in Utah provided a unique backdrop to Shari's formative years. The Franke family's home was filled with the sounds of laughter, bustling activity, and the occasional chaos that accompanies a large family. Despite the ordinary challenges of raising six children, the Franke household was a hub of love and learning. Shari, as the eldest child, often found herself balancing the dual roles of daughter and role model, setting the stage for the leadership qualities that would later define her journey.

The state's rich cultural tapestry also played a significant role in shaping Shari's early experiences. Influenced by Utah's predominantly Latter-day Saint (LDS) community, her upbringing was deeply intertwined with principles of faith, service, and resilience. These values were instilled in her from a young age and became a cornerstone of her identity, even as she faced the complexities of life in the public eye.

Family Traditions and Values

The Franke family's life was built on a strong foundation of traditions and values that fostered a sense of unity and purpose. Regular family gatherings, shared meals, and faith-based practices were at the core of their household. Sundays were particularly significant, often reserved for church services and moments of reflection. These routines not only strengthened their bonds but also provided a framework for navigating life's challenges.

Education and self-discipline were emphasized in the Franke home. Shari's parents, Ruby and Kevin, were dedicated to creating an environment where their children could thrive academically and personally. Family projects, collaborative activities, and moments of shared responsibility were designed to instill a sense of accountability and teamwork.

Yet, it wasn't all about structure and discipline. The Franke household also embraced creativity and playfulness. Holidays were marked by elaborate celebrations, complete with traditions that reflected their unique family dynamics. Whether it was decorating the Christmas tree, participating in neighborhood events, or crafting homemade gifts, these moments created lasting memories that shaped Shari's understanding of love and togetherness.

At the heart of the family's values was a commitment to fostering resilience. Life, as Ruby and Kevin often reminded their children, would not always be easy. Challenges were inevitable, but they were also opportunities for growth. This perspective, taught through both words and example, laid the groundwork for Shari's ability to navigate the hurdles she would later face in life.

As we delve deeper into Shari's story, it becomes clear that her upbringing in Utah and the traditions of her family were more than just the backdrop of her early years. They were the foundation upon which she began to build a life defined by resilience, creativity, and transformation.

2. THE BIRTH OF 8 PASSENGERS

Entering the Spotlight

The launch of *8 Passengers* marked a turning point not just for Shari Franke but for the entire Franke family. What began as a creative outlet quickly evolved into a full-fledged YouTube sensation, drawing millions of viewers from around the world. Ruby and Kevin Franke, Shari's parents, initially envisioned the channel as a way to document their family's day-to-day lives. However, its rapid popularity turned their modest project into one of the most recognized family vlogging channels of its time.

For Shari, entering the spotlight as part of *8 Passengers* was both an opportunity and a challenge. As the eldest of six siblings, she naturally became a focal point in the videos, often taking on a leadership role both on and off camera. Her personality, wit, and authenticity resonated with audiences, making her a favorite among viewers. Shari's academic achievements, personal milestones, and everyday interactions were often highlighted, giving fans a glimpse into her world.

However, the rapid rise to fame came with its own set of pressures. Filming was no longer an occasional activity; it became a daily routine. The line between private moments and public content blurred, and Shari found herself navigating the unique challenges of growing up in front of an audience. While she valued the opportunity to connect with viewers, she also began to feel the weight of being constantly watched and judged.

Family Dynamics on Camera

The success of *8 Passengers* brought the Franke family closer in some ways, but it also exposed them to new tensions and dynamics. On camera, the family was often portrayed as a cohesive unit, bound by shared values and traditions. Viewers were drawn to the seemingly relatable chaos of managing a household with six children, and the channel's content ranged from lighthearted vlogs to more serious discussions about parenting and faith.

Behind the scenes, however, the dynamics were more complex. The demands of maintaining a successful YouTube channel required constant planning, coordination, and participation from every family member. While some siblings thrived in the spotlight, others struggled with the loss of privacy and the pressure to perform for an audience.

Shari's role within the family was particularly nuanced. As the eldest, she often found herself in a position of responsibility, helping her younger siblings navigate their own experiences in the public eye. At the same time, she had her own challenges to face—balancing her personal development with the expectations placed upon her as both a daughter and a key figure in the channel's success.

As *8 Passengers* grew, so did the scrutiny. Viewers and critics began to analyze every aspect of the family's lives, from parenting decisions to interpersonal relationships. Shari, who was developing her own identity and values, began to question certain aspects of the channel's portrayal of their lives. This introspection marked the beginning of her journey toward greater independence, as she sought to establish boundaries and define her own path outside of the family narrative.

The birth of *8 Passengers* was a defining chapter in Shari Franke's life. It brought fame, opportunities, and unforgettable experiences, but it also set the stage for the challenges she would face as she began to step out of the spotlight and into her own story. Her journey beyond the camera would ultimately be one of resilience, self-discovery, and the pursuit of authenticity.

3. SHARI'S CHILDHOOD BEHIND THE SCENES

Balancing Public and Private Life

For Shari Franke, growing up behind the lens of *8 Passengers* was a unique experience, unlike that of most children her age. While many of her peers were focused on schoolwork, extracurricular activities, and making friends, Shari had an additional layer of responsibility—being part of a family that shared their lives with millions of viewers. This dual existence required her to balance the public persona of a YouTube star with her private identity as a young girl navigating the complexities of childhood and adolescence.

The Franke household was rarely without a camera. Everyday activities, from breakfast routines to family outings, were potential content for the channel. Shari often had to switch seamlessly between being a regular teenager and being a figure in a globally recognized narrative. This balancing act was no easy feat. While she appreciated the opportunity to connect with viewers and share her story, there were moments when she longed for privacy and the freedom to grow without the watchful eyes of an audience.

School provided a temporary escape from the digital spotlight. It was one of the few spaces where Shari could focus on academics, develop friendships, and explore her interests away from the pressures of being filmed. However, even in these environments, her YouTube fame sometimes followed her, as classmates and teachers recognized her from the channel. This blend of public and private life shaped Shari's perspective early on, teaching her the importance of boundaries and the value of carving out spaces for herself amid the whirlwind of online fame.

Early Signs of Independence

Despite her role within the family and the channel, Shari's independent spirit was evident from a young age. She was a natural leader, often stepping up to support her siblings and manage responsibilities within the household. Yet, this leadership wasn't just about helping others—it was also a reflection of her desire to chart her own course and make decisions that aligned with her values.

Shari's curiosity and drive pushed her to explore areas of life that extended beyond the family's vlogging endeavors. She excelled academically and pursued extracurricular activities that allowed her to develop her skills and interests. Whether it was participating in school clubs, excelling in her studies, or taking on community service projects, Shari consistently demonstrated a willingness to step outside of her comfort zone and embrace new challenges.

Her early signs of independence also manifested in her thoughtful reflections on the role of the channel in her life.

As she grew older, Shari began to question the implications of sharing so much of herself and her family with the public. These internal dialogues, though challenging, marked the beginning of her journey toward self-discovery. She started to consider what life might look like beyond the camera, planting the seeds for the eventual decisions that would redefine her path.

Even as a child, Shari displayed a maturity that belied her age. Her ability to balance the demands of public life with her private aspirations was a testament to her resilience and determination. These early experiences laid the foundation for the transformation she would undergo in her later years, as she stepped out of the family spotlight and into a life defined by her own choices.

4. THE RISE OF 8 PASSENGERS

Capturing Family Moments

The birth of *8 Passengers* in 2015 was a watershed moment for the Franke family, catapulting them into the digital spotlight. What started as a modest attempt to document everyday family life soon evolved into a YouTube phenomenon, drawing millions of subscribers and billions of views. Ruby Franke, the family matriarch, served as the face of the channel, but it was the genuine and relatable dynamics of the family that captivated audiences. From birthday celebrations to road trips, every moment became part of a narrative that blended entertainment with the reality of raising six children.

For viewers, *8 Passengers* offered an intimate glimpse into a seemingly ordinary family with extraordinary relatability. The channel resonated with audiences who found comfort, humor, and even inspiration in the Frankes' day-to-day life. Parents saw reflections of their own struggles and triumphs, while children related to the sibling dynamics and shared experiences of growing up.

The process of capturing these moments, however, required careful orchestration. Behind the lens, the Franke family worked tirelessly to maintain consistency, crafting content that struck a balance between candidness and storytelling. This often meant filming even during personal or challenging times, leading to a unique intersection of public transparency and private reality. For Shari, this dynamic was both rewarding and challenging, as she learned to navigate the fine line between sharing her life and preserving her sense of self.

Shari's Role as the Eldest Sibling

As the eldest of the six Franke children, Shari played a pivotal role in the *8 Passengers* narrative. Her presence brought a sense of stability and leadership to the channel, and she quickly became a fan favorite. Viewers were drawn to her maturity, wit, and authenticity, which stood out amid the family's often chaotic dynamics.

Shari's role extended beyond what was seen on camera. As the oldest sibling, she was frequently looked to as a role model by her younger brothers and sisters. Whether it was helping with homework, guiding her siblings through personal challenges, or simply providing a listening ear, Shari's sense of responsibility was evident. Her ability to balance this leadership role with her own needs and aspirations was remarkable, especially given the added pressure of public scrutiny.

On the channel, Shari's milestones were often celebrated in detail, from academic achievements to personal growth moments. These glimpses into her life made her relatable to viewers who were navigating similar phases of adolescence.

However, the spotlight also came with challenges, as Shari sometimes found herself struggling to reconcile the image presented to the world with her private reality.

Despite these challenges, Shari's role as the eldest sibling allowed her to cultivate skills and traits that would serve her well in her future endeavors. Leadership, resilience, and the ability to connect with others became defining characteristics of her personality. Her experiences during the rise of *8 Passengers* laid the groundwork for the person she would become—someone who could inspire others not just through her family's story but through her own journey of growth and transformation.

5. THE CHALLENGES OF INTERNET FAME

Public Scrutiny and Online Criticism

With the rise of *8 Passengers* came not only an increase in fame but also the harsh realities of public scrutiny. The Franke family quickly became a fixture in the YouTube landscape, attracting millions of views and a loyal following. However, with visibility came judgment, and Shari, like the rest of her family, found herself under a microscope.

The internet is a platform that thrives on commentary and opinions, often shared without a filter. For Shari, the constant influx of praise and criticism was overwhelming. While many fans showered her and her family with love and support, there was an equally vocal segment of the audience who felt entitled to weigh in on every detail of their lives. Personal decisions, parenting styles, and even the most mundane family activities were scrutinized and critiqued in ways that were often harsh and unforgiving.

Shari, in particular, was subject to intense online criticism. As a young girl growing up in the public eye, she was regularly the subject of both positive and negative comments. Her appearance, behavior, and even her personal growth were open for discussion, often by people who had no understanding of her reality. The criticisms ranged from trivial matters to deeply personal attacks, making it difficult for Shari to separate her identity from the commentary about her.

The pressure of constantly being watched, evaluated, and criticized began to take its toll. What started as a creative outlet for the Franke family became a battleground of public opinion. Shari and her siblings had to adjust to the idea that every part of their lives was now public, leading to a sense of vulnerability and, at times, alienation.

Coping with Pressure and Expectations

Amid the whirlwind of internet fame, Shari faced the enormous task of learning to cope with the pressure and expectations placed on her. As a teenager, she was still developing her sense of self, navigating the complexities of adolescence, and trying to figure out who she was outside of the family dynamic and the YouTube channel. Yet, the public had high expectations for her, often seeing her as a role model without fully understanding the challenges she was facing behind the scenes.

Shari's ability to cope with this pressure was shaped by both her upbringing and the support system around her. The values instilled in her by her parents—resilience, faith, and integrity—helped her weather the storm. However, coping wasn't always easy. There were moments when Shari questioned her role in the family and the channel, wondering if the public's perception of her was authentic or merely a projection of their own expectations.

To manage the mental and emotional strain, Shari learned to create boundaries. This wasn't just about separating her personal life from her public life; it was about protecting her sense of self. She began to distance herself from negative online commentary and focused on her own journey of growth. The journey wasn't linear, and there were many times when the weight of the pressure felt overwhelming, but Shari's inner strength and determination to find her own voice kept her moving forward.

Additionally, Shari relied on her family for support. While *8 Passengers* was a shared experience, each family member had their own way of coping with the pressures of internet fame. Together, they helped one another process the criticism, reinforcing the importance of family solidarity in the face of adversity.

The challenges of internet fame were undoubtedly difficult for Shari. Yet, these experiences shaped her resilience and ability to persevere through the storms of public life. Over time, she came to realize that while the world might have opinions about her, those opinions did not define her worth. She began to take control of her narrative, focusing less on external judgment and more on her own growth and happiness.

6. FINDING HER VOICE

Expressing Identity Amid the Spotlight

As Shari Franke navigated the pressures of growing up in the public eye, she began to realize that in order to move forward in a healthy and authentic way, she needed to find and express her true identity. Being thrust into the spotlight at such a young age meant that many of her formative years were shaped by the expectations and perceptions of others. As part of *8 Passengers*, she had always been seen through the lens of family dynamics, often defined by her role as the eldest sibling, the responsible one, the "good girl." But Shari was starting to feel that her true self was more complex than the image that had been cultivated for her.

For years, Shari's life had been largely shaped by the framework of the family channel—her personality, decisions, and aspirations were all filtered through that lens. As she matured, however, Shari began to question this narrative. She understood the need to carve out her own voice in the world, a voice that was distinct from the family brand that had dominated her existence. The process of finding that voice wasn't easy, and it required Shari to reconcile the pressure of living up to public expectations with the necessity of remaining true to herself.

One of the ways Shari began to express her evolving identity was through her increasing presence on social media. While

8 Passengers showcased a highly curated version of her life, Shari began to share her thoughts and experiences on her personal platforms. This shift allowed her to connect with her followers on a deeper level, offering a more nuanced view of who she was—beyond the camera and beyond the scripted moments of family vlogs. It wasn't just about the filtered moments of her life anymore; Shari shared the authentic highs and lows that many could relate to.

Her journey toward self-expression was also marked by a shift in her relationship with the public. As she began to assert her individuality, she found herself less concerned with conforming to others' expectations and more focused on embracing her own desires and aspirations. She explored different interests and passions, from studying psychology to focusing on self-care, and allowed her personality to shine through in ways that felt genuine to her. This wasn't a rejection of her family or the channel that had brought her fame, but rather an assertion that her identity as an individual was just as important as her role in the family dynamic.

Moments of Vulnerability and Growth

As Shari stepped into her own, the journey was not without its challenges. In fact, the process of finding her voice often brought her face to face with deep vulnerability. While the public persona she had built over the years was one of confidence and strength, the truth was that Shari struggled with the same doubts, insecurities, and questions that many young people face.

Her vulnerability became evident in moments of introspection, when she questioned the life she had built for herself and the decisions that lay ahead. The pressure to maintain a certain image on social media and within the confines of *8 Passengers* sometimes left her feeling disconnected from her authentic self. The vulnerability Shari experienced wasn't always visible to the public, but it was a crucial part of her growth process.

During these moments of self-reflection, Shari began to understand the importance of embracing imperfection. She no longer felt the need to meet external expectations or strive for an idealized version of success. Instead, she embraced the idea that true growth comes from embracing one's flaws, learning from mistakes, and evolving over time. Shari's personal growth, though not always linear, allowed her to better navigate the pressures of being in the spotlight while staying grounded in her personal values.

This period of vulnerability also led to Shari becoming more open about her emotional well-being and the challenges she faced. She shared candid moments about her struggles with mental health, body image, and identity, opening a dialogue that resonated deeply with her followers. By sharing her vulnerabilities, Shari gave others permission to do the same, creating a safe space for discussions about the complexities of growing up and finding one's place in the world.

These moments of vulnerability were not weaknesses; rather, they were opportunities for Shari to grow, learn, and ultimately become stronger. She realized that embracing her vulnerability was a key part of her personal evolution and an integral step in finding her voice. Through these experiences, Shari discovered that true strength comes not from perfection, but from being open, authentic, and unapologetically oneself.

7. LEAVING THE NEST

Pursuing Higher Education

For Shari Franke, leaving home and pursuing higher education marked a pivotal turning point in her journey toward independence. After years of growing up in the spotlight, she longed for a life that was her own—a life not dictated by filming schedules or the expectations of millions of viewers. College provided the perfect opportunity for Shari to step away from the structured environment of her family and explore her identity as an individual.

Choosing to study at Brigham Young University (BYU), a school deeply rooted in her family's values and faith, was a deliberate decision for Shari. It was a space where she could maintain the foundation of her upbringing while simultaneously stepping into new experiences and environments. College life offered her the freedom to meet new people, engage in intellectual challenges, and explore personal interests that she hadn't fully pursued during her time on *8 Passengers*.

Academically, Shari gravitated toward subjects that aligned with her desire to better understand people and relationships, including psychology and human development. She found fulfillment in her studies, which allowed her to grow intellectually while also giving her tools to navigate her own personal challenges. This academic journey was more than just a pursuit of knowledge—it was an avenue for Shari to redefine herself outside the shadow of her family's public persona.

College also introduced Shari to a more diverse range of perspectives. For someone who had grown up in a close-knit, somewhat insulated environment, this exposure was both enlightening and transformative. It challenged her to think critically about her own values, beliefs, and goals, enabling her to form a clearer sense of who she wanted to become.

Life Beyond the Camera

Transitioning from a life lived largely on camera to one of relative anonymity was a significant adjustment for Shari. For much of her adolescence, the routines of daily life had been intertwined with the demands of running a YouTube channel. Every moment—from mundane tasks to monumental milestones—was captured, edited, and shared with millions. Leaving that life behind required Shari to relearn how to exist in a way that felt natural and unobserved.

In many ways, this transition was liberating. For the first time in years, Shari had the chance to experience life without the constant presence of an audience. She could make mistakes, try new things, and explore her identity without worrying about how it would be perceived by the public. This newfound freedom allowed her to engage in activities she had once avoided or overlooked, from joining campus clubs to building friendships based on shared interests rather than shared fame.

However, the shift wasn't without its challenges. After years of being in the public eye, stepping away from the spotlight came with a sense of loss and disorientation. The rhythm of her life had changed dramatically, and she had to confront the question of who she was without the constant validation—or criticism—of an audience. This period of adjustment required Shari to dig deep, leaning on her inner strength and the lessons she had learned from her experiences in the spotlight.

Gradually, Shari began to find joy in the simplicity of a more private life. She discovered that the absence of constant public attention allowed her to focus on relationships and personal growth in a way that hadn't been possible before. Life beyond the camera became an opportunity for Shari to prioritize her own well-being, set boundaries, and cultivate a sense of independence that would serve her well in the years to come.

By leaving the nest, Shari not only gained physical distance from the world of *8 Passengers,* but she also took a significant step toward reclaiming her narrative. College and life beyond the camera became a sanctuary for growth, self-discovery, and empowerment, setting the stage for the next chapter of her journey.

8. REDEFINING RELATIONSHIPS

Navigating Family Tensions

As Shari Franke stepped into her independence, the shifting dynamics within her family became more pronounced. Growing up in the public eye as part of *8 Passengers,* her relationships with her parents and siblings were shaped by the pressures of maintaining a cohesive on-screen image. However, as she matured, Shari began to question aspects of her upbringing and the values that had been emphasized in the household.

The Franke family's decision to share their lives on YouTube came with immense scrutiny, and over time, cracks began to form behind the seemingly perfect facade. Shari's transition to adulthood brought to light differences in perspectives and values between her and her parents, particularly regarding the handling of their public life. While Shari valued authenticity and personal growth, she struggled with how her family's public persona sometimes clashed with her evolving sense of self.

Family tensions were not limited to philosophical differences; they were also fueled by the unique challenges of living in the public eye. The pressures of constantly being watched, judged, and critiqued by millions often created an environment where open communication was difficult. Shari found herself navigating the complexities of expressing her concerns without undermining her loyalty to her family—a delicate balance that required maturity and courage.

Though tensions were inevitable, Shari recognized the importance of maintaining love and respect for her family. This did not mean ignoring the challenges but rather addressing them with compassion and understanding. For Shari, navigating family tensions was less about seeking resolution for every conflict and more about finding peace within herself.

The Decision to Speak Out

One of the most defining moments in Shari's journey was her decision to publicly address her experiences within the Franke household. This decision was not made lightly. Speaking out meant opening up old wounds, exposing vulnerabilities, and potentially straining relationships further. However, Shari felt a deep sense of responsibility—not only to herself but also to others who might benefit from her honesty.

For years, Shari had remained relatively silent about the challenges she faced growing up in a highly visible and structured environment. While her public persona often reflected confidence and composure, she harbored feelings and stories that had yet to be shared. Over time, she realized that withholding these truths was not only stifling her personal growth but also perpetuating a narrative that no longer aligned with her reality.

Shari's decision to speak out came with risks. She knew her words would be scrutinized, and her intentions might be misunderstood. Yet, she was driven by a desire to reclaim her narrative and to shed light on the pressures and complexities of growing up in a public family. Her voice became a beacon of authenticity, offering a nuanced perspective that resonated with many who had experienced similar struggles in their own lives.

In interviews, social media posts, and other platforms, Shari shared her journey with honesty and vulnerability. She spoke about the impact of constant public scrutiny, the challenges of navigating family relationships in such a high-pressure environment, and her path to healing and self-discovery. Her words were not intended to place blame but to offer insight into the realities of a life that had often been idealized by viewers.

Shari's decision to speak out was also an act of empowerment. It allowed her to take control of her story and to use her experiences as a catalyst for change. By sharing her truth, she not only redefined her relationship with her audience but also demonstrated the power of vulnerability and resilience.

In redefining her relationships—both with her family and with the public—Shari emerged as a voice of authenticity and strength. She showed that while family bonds may be tested, the process of addressing and understanding those challenges can lead to growth, healing, and transformation.

9. THE HOUSE OF MY MOTHER: A JOURNEY OF REFLECTION

Shari's Inspirational Debut Book

The House of My Mother marked a profound milestone in Shari Franke's journey—her debut as an author and a storyteller. The book was far more than a collection of memories or reflections; it was a testament to her resilience, creativity, and ability to transform personal experiences into universal lessons. Through her writing, Shari invited readers into the depths of her heart and mind, offering a vulnerable yet empowering narrative about self-discovery, healing, and growth.

The title, *The House of My Mother*, served as a metaphor for Shari's exploration of her identity, rooted in the complexities of her upbringing. The "house" represented the foundational values, lessons, and experiences passed down by her mother, while also symbolizing the challenges and limitations she had to confront as she grew into her own person. Through poignant storytelling, Shari dissected the duality of her family life—the warmth and love that defined her childhood, juxtaposed with the pressures and expectations that came with being part of a public family.

Shari's writing struck a balance between reflection and inspiration. She delved into deeply personal moments, sharing the struggles of navigating relationships, the pain of feeling misunderstood, and the triumphs of reclaiming her voice. Her narrative resonated with readers not only because of its authenticity but also because it shed light on universal themes—identity, resilience, and the pursuit of self-worth.

The book's release was met with widespread praise for its raw honesty and thoughtful prose. Readers were moved by Shari's ability to articulate emotions that many had felt but struggled to express. Critics highlighted her skill in weaving personal anecdotes with broader insights, creating a work that was both intimate and universally relatable. For Shari, *The House of My Mother* was not just a book; it was a bridge between her past and future, a way to honor where she came from while carving out her own path forward.

Personal Growth Through Writing

The process of writing *The House of My Mother* became a transformative journey for Shari. As she sat down to pen her story, she found herself revisiting moments she had long tucked away—some joyous, others painful, but all integral to her growth. The act of writing allowed her to process these experiences in a way she never had before, providing clarity and closure where it had previously eluded her.

Through her writing, Shari discovered a profound sense of empowerment. The ability to frame her narrative on her own terms was a stark contrast to the years she spent living under the public's gaze, where her story was often shaped by external perceptions. Writing gave her the opportunity to reclaim her voice and tell her truth, unfiltered and unapologetic.

The process wasn't without its challenges. Revisiting painful memories required emotional vulnerability, and there were moments when Shari questioned whether she was ready to share so much of herself with the world. However, she found strength in the knowledge that her story could inspire others. By embracing her vulnerability, she created a space where readers could feel seen, understood, and encouraged to embark on their own journeys of self-discovery.

The House of My Mother also deepened Shari's understanding of herself. The introspection required to write such a personal work helped her identify patterns, heal wounds, and celebrate victories she had previously overlooked. Writing became a form of therapy, a way to make sense of her past while laying the foundation for her future.

As the book reached readers around the world, Shari was overwhelmed by the connections it fostered. Letters, comments, and messages poured in from people who found pieces of their own stories within her pages. The book's impact reaffirmed Shari's belief in the power of storytelling to bridge divides and spark meaningful change.

In the end, *The House of My Mother* was more than a book—it was a declaration of selfhood, a testament to resilience, and an invitation for others to reflect on their own lives. It marked the beginning of a new chapter for Shari, one where her voice, creativity, and courage could shine without limitation.

10. BUILDING A LIFE OF INDEPENDENCE

Academic Achievements and Goals

For Shari Franke, building a life of independence began with a strong commitment to academic excellence and personal growth. Her college years at Brigham Young University (BYU) served as the foundation for this transformation, where she immersed herself in subjects that challenged her mind and fueled her passions. Pursuing a major that aligned with her interest in understanding people and relationships—such as psychology or human development—Shari found fulfillment in both the intellectual rigor and the personal insights gained through her studies.

Education became a crucial tool for Shari to redefine herself outside the shadow of her family's YouTube legacy. It offered her the opportunity to craft a vision for her future that was entirely her own, built on her values, interests, and aspirations. She set ambitious goals for herself, determined to use her education not only to advance her career but also to make a meaningful impact in the world.

As a student, Shari demonstrated resilience and discipline, excelling in her coursework while also navigating the pressures of transitioning to an independent life. The structure and challenge of academic life taught her valuable lessons in time management, critical thinking, and self-reliance. Beyond the classroom, she participated in campus activities and social organizations, forging connections with peers who supported and inspired her growth.

Her academic journey was not without its challenges. Balancing the demands of higher education with the emotional complexities of distancing herself from her past required tremendous inner strength. Yet, Shari embraced these difficulties as opportunities for growth, viewing each obstacle as a stepping stone toward a life defined by her choices and values.

The Shift Toward Advocacy and Awareness

As Shari gained independence, she began to embrace a deeper sense of purpose: advocating for awareness around mental health, family dynamics, and the pressures of life in the public eye. Drawing from her personal experiences, Shari felt a responsibility to use her platform to foster understanding and support for those facing similar struggles.

Through social media, public speaking, and community engagement, Shari started to share her insights on topics that were both deeply personal and universally relevant. She opened up about the challenges of growing up in a high-profile family, the emotional toll of constant public scrutiny, and the importance of mental health awareness. Her vulnerability and authenticity resonated with her audience, many of whom found comfort and validation in her words. Shari's advocacy was not limited to sharing her story; she actively sought ways to create change. She collaborated with organizations focused on mental health, family counseling, and online safety, lending her voice and resources to initiatives aimed at education and support. Her efforts were driven by a desire to empower others to navigate their own challenges with courage and resilience.

This shift toward advocacy also marked a significant transformation in how Shari viewed her past. Rather than seeing her experiences as burdens, she reframed them as tools for growth and connection. By sharing her journey, she hoped to break down stigmas, encourage open conversations, and inspire others to seek healing and self-empowerment.

In building a life of independence, Shari Franke demonstrated that resilience is not about erasing the past but about learning from it and using those lessons to shape a better future. Her academic achievements and advocacy work stood as testaments to her determination to live authentically and make a positive impact on the world around her.

11. FAITH, CREATIVITY, AND PURPOSE

Shari's Personal Beliefs and Their Influence

Faith has always been a cornerstone of Shari Franke's life, shaping her perspective and guiding her decisions. Growing up in a deeply religious household, she was immersed in the teachings and values of The Church of Jesus Christ of Latter-day Saints (LDS Church) from an early age. These principles influenced her sense of morality, family values, and resilience, even as she later began to explore her own interpretation of spirituality and faith.

As Shari matured, her relationship with faith evolved. While she valued the foundational teachings she grew up with, she sought a deeper, more personal connection to her beliefs. Moving away from the structured environment of her childhood gave her the opportunity to question, reflect, and ultimately redefine her spirituality in a way that aligned with her growing independence. This exploration became a source of strength, offering her a sense of purpose and peace amid the challenges of life in the public eye.

Faith also played a significant role in Shari's healing process. During times of doubt and adversity, she turned to prayer, meditation, and scripture for guidance. Her belief in a higher purpose helped her navigate complex emotions, providing a framework for forgiveness, understanding, and personal growth. Over time, Shari's faith became a tool for empowerment rather than a set of rigid expectations, allowing her to live authentically while staying true to her spiritual roots.

Shari's journey with faith wasn't just about personal transformation; it also inspired her to support others in their spiritual paths. She used her platform to encourage conversations about faith, identity, and the importance of staying open to change. Her willingness to share her evolving beliefs resonated with many, showing that spirituality can be a dynamic and deeply personal journey.

Exploring Her Artistic and Creative Side

Creativity has always been an integral part of Shari's identity, offering her an outlet for self-expression and a way to process her experiences. Whether through writing, art, or other creative endeavors, Shari found joy and fulfillment in exploring her imaginative side.

One of the most prominent expressions of her creativity was her debut book, *The House of My Mother*. Writing became a therapeutic and transformative process for Shari, allowing her to articulate emotions and stories that had shaped her life. The book's success not only showcased her talent as a writer but also highlighted her ability to connect with readers on a deeply emotional level.

Beyond writing, Shari also explored other artistic pursuits, such as painting, photography, and music. These creative outlets became a sanctuary for her—a space where she could disconnect from the pressures of the outside world and immerse herself in the act of creation. Through her art, Shari found a way to channel her emotions, celebrate her individuality, and explore themes of resilience, identity, and transformation.

Creativity also became a bridge between Shari and her audience. She often shared glimpses of her artistic projects on social media, inspiring others to embrace their own creative passions. Her openness about the importance of art in her healing journey encouraged her followers to see creativity as a powerful tool for self-discovery and empowerment.

For Shari, creativity was more than a hobby; it was a form of purpose. It allowed her to tell her story, connect with others, and leave a lasting impact on the world. Through her faith and creativity, she discovered a sense of balance and fulfillment, proving that personal growth and artistic expression are deeply intertwined.

12. EMPOWERING OTHERS

Messages of Hope and Resilience

One of the most profound aspects of Shari Franke's transformation was her unwavering commitment to spreading hope and resilience. Having faced a unique set of challenges growing up in the public eye, Shari understood the weight of criticism, the complexities of family dynamics, and the struggle to find self-worth in a world that often demands perfection. Her experiences became the foundation for a mission: to empower others by sharing her journey authentically and vulnerably.

Through interviews, social media, and public appearances, Shari shared personal stories of triumph over adversity. She spoke candidly about her battles with self-doubt, the pressures of fame, and the emotional toll of stepping away from her family's public image. By openly addressing these struggles, Shari created a safe space for others to feel seen and understood. Her messages often focused on the idea that resilience is not about avoiding challenges but about facing them with courage and learning from them.

Shari's words carried a sense of relatability and optimism. She emphasized that healing and personal growth are lifelong journeys, filled with ups and downs but always worth pursuing. Her audience—many of whom faced their own battles with identity, family, or societal expectations—found comfort and inspiration in her ability to turn pain into strength.

Beyond her personal story, Shari advocated for mental health awareness and emotional well-being, urging her followers to seek help when needed and prioritize their own happiness. Her message was clear: everyone has the power to rewrite their narrative, no matter how challenging their circumstances may be.

Inspiring Young Women to Embrace Change

Shari's journey from a young girl navigating the pressures of internet fame to an independent, empowered woman resonated deeply with young women around the world. She became a role model for embracing change, showing that growth often requires stepping out of one's comfort zone and confronting difficult truths.

Through her platforms, Shari encouraged young women to challenge societal expectations and embrace their individuality. She spoke about the importance of self-discovery and the need to prioritize one's values and passions over external validation. Whether discussing her decision to leave her family's YouTube channel or her pursuit of higher education and creative passions, Shari consistently highlighted the importance of taking control of one's own narrative.

Shari also addressed issues that are particularly relevant to young women, such as body image, self-esteem, and the pressure to conform. She advocated for self-acceptance and self-love, reminding her audience that true beauty lies in authenticity and confidence. Her messages often included actionable advice, such as journaling, setting personal boundaries, and surrounding oneself with supportive people who encourage growth.

Her advocacy extended beyond words. Shari collaborated with organizations and initiatives aimed at empowering young women, offering workshops, mentorship, and resources to help them navigate life's transitions. These efforts reflected her belief that every young woman has the potential to overcome challenges and create a meaningful life, no matter their background or circumstances.

For Shari, empowering others was not just about sharing her story; it was about creating a ripple effect of positivity and change. By inspiring young women to embrace their unique journeys, she helped pave the way for a generation that values authenticity, resilience, and the courage to grow.

13. THE IMPACT OF HER JOURNEY

Reflections on Fame, Family, and Freedom

Shari Franke's life story is one of transformation, resilience, and the pursuit of authenticity. From her early days as a public figure in *8 Passengers* to her emergence as an independent and empowered individual, her journey has left a lasting impact not only on her own life but also on the lives of countless others who have followed her story.

For Shari, fame was a double-edged sword. It brought opportunities and visibility but also subjected her to intense scrutiny and criticism. Reflecting on this chapter of her life, Shari acknowledges the challenges that came with living in the spotlight, including the loss of privacy and the pressure to present a curated image of perfection. However, she also recognizes how these experiences shaped her character, teaching her the importance of resilience, self-awareness, and the courage to break free from societal expectations.

Her relationship with family remains a complex and evolving part of her story. Growing up in a highly visible and tightly-knit family brought both joy and tension, as the boundaries between personal and public life often blurred. Shari's decision to step away from her family's YouTube channel and carve out her own path was a defining moment in her journey, symbolizing her commitment to living authentically. Despite the challenges, Shari reflects on her family dynamics with a sense of gratitude for the lessons learned and a hope for healing and understanding in the future.

Freedom, for Shari, came through self-discovery and the pursuit of her passions. Whether through education, creative expression, or advocacy, she found liberation in embracing her individuality and living life on her own terms. Her reflections on fame, family, and freedom serve as a testament to the power of personal growth and the importance of staying true to oneself.

14. LOOKING AHEAD

Shari's Vision for the Future

As Shari Franke looks to the future, her vision is shaped by the lessons of her past and the aspirations she has cultivated through her journey of self-discovery. Having emerged from the shadows of her family's public life, she is determined to carve out a path that reflects her values, passions, and newfound independence.

Education remains a central pillar of her plans, with Shari focusing on completing her studies and applying her knowledge to meaningful endeavors. Her academic pursuits, particularly in fields like psychology, human development, or creative writing, are not merely a means to a career but a way to deepen her understanding of herself and the world around her. Shari envisions using her education to make a tangible difference, whether through professional advocacy, counseling, or creative projects that inspire and empower others.

Creativity will continue to play a vital role in her future. Following the success of her debut book, *The House of My Mother,* Shari plans to expand her repertoire as an author and artist. She is exploring ideas for future books, including memoirs, novels, and works that focus on personal growth and resilience. In addition, she has expressed interest in branching into other creative mediums, such as visual arts or documentary filmmaking, to share stories that resonate with her audience on a deeper level.

At the heart of Shari's vision is a commitment to advocacy and community. She hopes to use her platform to amplify important causes, including mental health awareness, family support systems, and empowering young women to embrace change. Whether through public speaking engagements, collaborations with organizations, or grassroots initiatives, Shari sees her future as one of service and connection.

The Ongoing Story of Transformation

Shari's journey is far from over. Her story is a testament to the idea that transformation is a continuous process, not a single destination. As she navigates new challenges and opportunities, she remains steadfast in her commitment to growth, authenticity, and resilience.

The themes of transformation are evident in every aspect of her life: her evolving relationship with her faith, her dedication to creative expression, and her efforts to redefine what it means to live a fulfilling life. For Shari, transformation is not about erasing the past but embracing it as a foundation for building a brighter future.

Shari's story continues to inspire those who follow her journey, as she proves that it is possible to rise above adversity and thrive on one's own terms. Whether she is writing, advocating, or simply living her truth, Shari's ongoing evolution serves as a beacon of hope for those seeking to find their own path.

As she looks ahead, Shari remains committed to her core values: faith, creativity, and purpose. With her ever-growing audience, she has the potential to leave an indelible mark not only on her community but also on the broader conversation around resilience, empowerment, and transformation.

Made in United States
Troutdale, OR
01/20/2025

28092507R00037